Critics Are Raving About the Thumbs Down Method

"The more you read about golf technique, the more you often become bogged down in meaningless jargon and excessive detail. So for me, Alan Martin's *Thumbs Down* method was an absolute revolution: it is clear, simple, mechanically sound … and IT WORKS!

Not only have my scores fallen, I now feel as if for the first time I have a sound, self-correcting understanding of the golf swing that I can take on the course with me and use at any time."

Landon Jones, Weekend Golfer
Former editor, *PEOPLE* magazine

"It's just Thumbs Up and *Thumbs Down*. What could be simpler?"

Ken Dashow, Radio Personality
Q1043 Classic Rock, NYC

T0126197

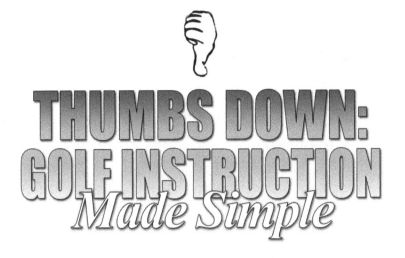

THUMBS DOWN: GOLF INSTRUCTION
Made Simple

The Thumbs Down Method:
A Golfer's How-To Guide for Better Ball Striking

Alan J. Martin

NEW YORK

Thumbs Down: Golf Instruction Made Simple

By Alan J. Martin

ISBN: 978-1-60037-445-6 Paperback

Published by:

MORGAN · JAMES
THE ENTREPRENEURIAL PUBLISHER™

Morgan James Publishing, LLC
1225 Franklin Ave Ste 325
Garden City, NY 11530-1693
Toll Free 800-485-4943
www.MorganJamesPublishing.com

Cover & Interior Design by:
Heather Kirk
www.GraphicsByHeather.com
Heather@GraphicsByHeather.com

Habitat
for Humanity®
Peninsula
Building Partner

Table of Contents

About the Author: Alan Martin

The Story of my Life and my Game

BEFORE YOU BEGIN reading this book, I'd be surprised if you didn't ask yourself questions like these:

- Who is Alan Martin?

- What kind of golfer is he?

- Why did he write this book, when there are dozens of books and teaching aids available from golf's best players and instructors?

- How will the *Thumbs Down* method help me?

- Why is the *Thumbs Down* method better for me than advice from the experts?

These are good and valid questions, all answered throughout this section. The next obvious one is why wouldn't I just go to a pro for help with my game? The simple answer is you could, and if you're a beginner you should. A solid foundation is important in any sport, especially golf.

This book was never intended as an anti-lesson or anti-pro gimmick. It's not the complete book of golf instruction or positioned as a substitute for taking lessons and learning the game from a certified PGA teaching professional. Traditional golf instruction never worked for me, but I respect and admire professional instructors, for the important role they play and all they do to improve the great game of golf. For me, it always came down to at least one of these three factors: time, money, or simplicity. The first two speak for themselves. I was never a big fan of taking lessons because it was very confusing and always seemed to focus too much on making the perfect swing.

It always puzzled me as I watched a comparison of pros swinging in slow motion. Anyone could easily see how different each player's swing was, as compared to the other. My eyes always zoomed in on the moment of truth in the golf swing, seeing how similar they all looked while striking the ball. It disturbed me every time the announcers glanced over the moment of impact, concentrating their explanations on the mechanics of the swing instead. My eyes glazed over with confusion, when the experts gave a detailed description of the player's swing, in a language only physics majors understand, not me. Almost everything I saw, heard, and read encouraged me to believe that consistent ball striking was the result of proper swing fundamentals, and centrifugal force squared the club naturally. Maybe it's natural for those who play and practice full-time, but for myself and the majority of recreational players I play with, there's nothing natural about it.

This book was written for the millions of serious amateurs who want to improve, with a passion. Even though the game of golf continues to gain in popularity, it's not growing in size. Personally, I believe the average Joe (male or female) is tired of not improving quickly enough, like the commercials guarantee. Golf is a difficult game to play and it requires years of learning to play it well. I can only imagine how confusing it is for newer golfers to learn and understand the complex terminology I often hear. Since finding answers in simple terms isn't easy, I felt I needed to share the simple method I discovered during the process of curing my own out-of-control slice.

Often controversial with golf pros, my message stresses the importance of using the hands to square the club at impact, as the top priority versus making a pretty swing. Since I live in an amateur's shoes everyday, I have a first-hand understanding of the challenges we face, that pros will never have. After experimenting on several willing amateurs and myself for years, it was easy to see how well the method worked and how easily golfers could teach it to themselves, in minutes. I was convinced. For fellow amateurs, the *Thumbs Down* method is the missing ingredient we've been looking for. Now it was time to throw my hat in the ring, with a method for the masses that worked and offered "simplicity at last".

What kept me motivated during a longer than expected process, was I knew I had something that could be really big, maybe even revolutionary. My research confirmed that the *Thumbs Down* method was based on the same ball striking fundamentals used by the best players and taught by top instructors, whether they know it or want to admit it. The light bulb finally went off in my mind, when for the first time there was a simple answer to my question, "what do I do now", just before the club strikes the ball. After years of desperately searching for the answer to that question, it came down to this thought; "just make a *Thumbs Down* at the golf ball as you strike it". What could be simpler?

My dream is that one day the *Thumbs Down* method will be recognized as the next big idea in golf and I'll be known as the golf expert for the average Joe. It might even launch my new writing and speaking career, combining my knowledge of golf and sales, called "turn golf into business". It's positioned to help men and women use the power of golf, to network and build relationships. The e-course will teach companies to use the golf course as the meeting room, where deals get done. What do you think? Stranger things have happened.

The remainder of this section tells my story from all angles, during many time periods. Please try to follow my real life roller coaster adventure, with an inside-the-ropes view of the outside-the-box solution that dramatically improved my golf game. Enjoy the ride and welcome to my world!

Alan Martin (the real me) was born in New York City in 1954, grew up and went to school on Long Island. Upon graduating from college, my career path took me into sales in 1977. Today I live in New Jersey, after moving and starting a family during the decade of the 1980s. With the exception of two years as a stock-broker, I worked in the computer industry. During the good and mostly challenging times, I was successful enough to afford a middle class living, as a regional salesman for many small software companies, until early 2006. Throughout those years, golf was the one constant in my life. It was also the only sport I continued to play on a regular basis. Even while coaching my children as they played youth sports, I found a way to support my habit of playing at least one weekend round of golf, nine months out of the year.

At five-foot, seven-inches and 150 pounds I was an unlikely future star in the NFL, but that didn't discourage or stop me from trying (between 1976 and 1979 I had six pro tryouts). Throughout my childhood

I played, watched or thought about sports constantly. I taught myself to play by watching on TV. Because I already played baseball and hockey, hitting a golf ball came naturally to me and lessons were never considered. Being an athlete was not only my passion; it's played a key role in shaping all aspects of my life. In fact, I credit the participation in sports for my competitive, do-it-yourselfer's attitude and entrepreneurial spirit.

After twenty-five years of playing golf, just finding the time to play, practice and maintain a single digit handicap was becoming a stretch. Now in my late thirties, with a full-time family life and career to manage, golf was more than just a game and passion. Golf was the only sport I still played competitively. It was my lifestyle and part of my DNA structure.

During the late 1980's life came at me fast, as all at once I was a new father with a career in transition. At the same time, my golf game mysteriously took a turn for the worse. I remember one depressing moment of weakness as it was hitting rock bottom, when I thought about giving up golf for a while. Down deep, I always believed the problem was only temporary, and soon I'd find the key to getting my old game back. As much as I wanted to enjoy myself, the golf game I was playing embarrassed and frustrated me more than ever before. Good, bad or ugly, I needed my weekly fix.

Everything happens for a reason, is an expression that fits. Call it fate or destiny, but the terrible golf seasons I had between 1989 and 1993 turned out to be the springboard for my future career change as a golf inventor, author and entrepreneur. Like most inventions, it all started with a problem that needed to be solved. In this case, self-preservation is a better description. If you're a serious golfer like me, you understand how much of a priority it was to fix my problem.

The WOW moment came in the summer of 1995. After years of searching for a solution, I officially fixed my ball striking problem one afternoon, by the club's practice green. Not only was it exciting, I realized I had just solved the same problem suffered by tens of millions of fellow amateur golfers, all around the world. The *Thumbs Down* method was priceless. It was so simple and revolutionary; I needed to share it with my fellow amateurs. It was like discovering the Holy Grail we've all been searching for.

For years, I thought just solving my golfing problem was the hard part. Now that I was thinking about writing a book about it and competing against the masters of golf instruction, the challenges grew rapidly. First and foremost, because I wasn't a pro and didn't have a name anyone recognized, my method had to work as advertised. Equally important, the product had to be positioned as something unique, without alien-ating myself from every PGA pro and instructor. I'm still not sure how that problem will ever be solved.

Let's rewind the clock back to 1964, when at the age of ten I was first introduced to golf. My immediate attraction was because of these main reasons:

- My love of sports

- I watched the final holes when Arnold Palmer won his forth Masters Tournament on TV

- I loved watching Shell's Wonderful World of Golf on my Aunt's new color TV

- My father played golf

- My older brother and his friends were also just beginning

That summer I picked up a golf club for the first time. In those days, golf meant hitting balls at a local school, with cut down clubs I shared with my brother. From the beginning, hitting the ball was easy for me, but keeping it from slicing to the right wasn't.

The following year my family bought a color TV. Cartoons, golf and a few shows were initially broadcast in color. As a fan of Arnold Palmer plus with the thrill of color, I enjoyed watching golf. A quick learner of sports, I taught myself to play by imitating Palmer, Gary Player and other pros I watched. Also, my next-door neighbor and best friend played golf. Since his family belonged to a golf and pool club, he took lessons and always shared his knowledge with me, as we hit balls at the school. These were the initial fundamentals I remember the most:

- Hold the club with an overlapping grip

- Bend the knees

- Keep your head down

- Keep the left arm straight

- Hit down on the ball

- Let the left side do all the work, while the right side goes along for the ride

- Follow-through

My friend also introduced me to a term called pronating, a key component of the golf swing used by pros after hitting the ball. Because it was difficult to understand and awkward to execute, I paid little attention. Ironically, pronating is the foundation concept of the *Thumbs Down* method.

At the age of eleven while attending summer camp, I played my first round of golf. Nine holes on a tiny home-made dirt course during our Color War competition, was where my initial love for playing the game began. Coincidentally, I scored my first (and only) hole-in-one ever during this event. It happened on the last hole, when my tee shot bounced up and grazed the flag. The rules counted it as an ace. Imagine the thrill, as it won the match for my team. I was officially hooked on golf.

Two years later I played for the first time on a real golf course. My friends and I played nine holes at local parks or at pitch and putt courses. My first eighteen-hole experience was planned during a family vacation to Florida, as my father and I teed off one hot and sunny morning. Gradually throughout the round, we noticed signs that warned about problems with mosquitoes. Determination and desire only goes so far, because after twelve holes the swarms forced us to race off the course. Back at our hotel, my mother counted over two hundred bites all over my body.

At that time, my father was a member at a golf club. He had a Saturday morning starting time, with a group he played with. When a member couldn't play, I occasionally filled in. At the age of fifteen, I scored in the low 100s, then steadily improved into the 90s (remember in golf, a lower score is better).

During the next few years I filled in more frequently, and my father never could beat me. Throughout high school and college I played about ten rounds a year, breaking 90 occasionally.

I could always hit a long ball, but with a fade or slice I couldn't always control where it went. Thanks to practice at the school as a beginner, my short game was good. Soon, rounds in the 80s became more frequent. Putting was a part of the game that always held me back. The problem started when I fell in love with the mallet putters I saw the pros use on TV in the 1960s. I'm not sure if the putter was the only problem, but I know I developed a lot of bad putting habits early.

My career success, allowed me to move out on my own in 1978, to an apartment outside of New York City. The nearby golf courses were in terrible shape and not much fun to play, so I played very little golf for a few years. It all changed in 1981 when I moved into my first home, a condominium in New Jersey. The change in scenery motivated me to get serious about playing golf, on a regular basis. To my delight, there were several nice public golf courses to choose from within a few miles of my new home.

Later that year, a major Wall Street firm recruited me to join them as a stockbroker. The career shift was responsible for my joining a country club, using the golf course for business purposes. A nearby club offered a first year try it policy, without any long-term commitments. I applied and joined in 1983. The course didn't suit my game, plus it just wasn't a good fit for other reasons. As I began asking around for alternatives in the area, I was invited to play a beautiful private course only ten miles away. Midway through the round I knew this was the club I really wanted to join. In October, I was paired with a member during a local Chamber of Commerce golf outing. He was more than happy to sponsor me for membership, beginning the next season.

In January, I won an incentive bonus for top achievers. The money only made the decision to join easier, because it paid my entire club initiation fee and first year's dues. I enjoyed playing this course and after a few years, was considered one of the better players. In 1987 I won my first golf tournament. It was the President's Cup, a match play tournament with full handicaps. This means there are individual competitions between different levels of players, where anyone can beat anyone. That's because the lower rated player gets strokes subtracted, to make up the differences in their average scores. At that time my game was in top form, playing to an eight handicap. That meant I posted scores averaging in the low 80s. Not bad for a once a week player with minimal practice time, who plays over 95 percent of his golf in his head!

When I lost my job in the spring of 1989, both my career and mental state were in need of repair. Married three years with a new house and a child, money problems were the last thing I needed, or so I thought. During that year, my fine-tuned golf game headed in the same direction. Without warning, my ball striking skills also abandoned me. My swing didn't feel comfortable and I lost distance with all my clubs, as the power fade sliced further to the right. I remember watching the Club Championship in July with the mother of one of the players. When she asked my how my game was, I said, "I've lost my swing and don't feel comfortable with my game". She looked puzzled because I had recently won a major tournament and had a reputation as a good player at the club.

My irons were by far the worst clubs in my bag. The harder I tried to hit the ball the more it sliced to the right. In addition to shorter drives, my iron shots lost well over twenty yards. The simple compact swing that produced long shots with a power fade suddenly produced ugly looking shots. The single digit handicap I had kept since joining the club slipped away, rising to a twelve by the end of the next year. Still answers why.

As the 1992 season began, I turned to the experts on TV and popular golf magazines for help. They all stressed the large muscles in the legs, hips, and shoulders for power. Focusing on these parts of my body now had the opposite effect for me. The decrease in distance only made me try to swing my body faster at the ball. One day I even drew this bizarre thought; if the spikes on my shoes were longer, I could get a better body turn into the shot. Another off-the-wall conclusion was that my clubs lost their power, because I was hitting the ball in the center of the club. My irons were actually women's clubs purchased from a fellow club member, who preferred lighter clubs. It was possible, but not likely.

One day, a letter in the mail offered a book written by a pro, sharing the secrets used by top money players. I bought it with the thought that the answer I was looking for would soon be found. I was dead wrong! Most of the information was very basic and the tips didn't help. In fact, the swing thoughts that worked for pros only confused me more. The drills didn't help and made my practice sessions less productive than before. Although I gave up on the book I liked its cartoon style format, with hand drawn illustrations and captions that told the story. I remember thinking if it was pocket-sized, I could bring it to the driving range and practice the drills, or have it with me on the course while I played.

The next brainstorm thought was to convert my irons to woods, because I could always hit a wood. My thinking was ten years ahead of its time, since the hybrids we have today weren't invented yet. As a start, I purchased a 12-wood (an 8-iron equivalent) through a specialty catalog, and tried it out on a few holes by myself one afternoon. The only shots I could hit were pop-ups. On our 126 yard fifteenth hole, I hit my shot short of the green. Right then I decided that I couldn't play like this and **had** to find a way to hit my irons better or give up the game, because this was embarrassing. I had hit rock bottom.

As a final act of desperation I took my first and only lesson from the club's assistant pro. In the past I resisted taking lessons, because I had an efficient swing that worked well, with no desire to change it. The hour we spent didn't cure my bad swing habits or slice. To this day I still can't understand what he was trying to get me to do, but I remember him using the term "plane" frequently. Maybe it's the magic swing thought for pros, but it wasn't for me. The experience taught me that pro's relate better to the problems of pros, than they do with the problems faced by amateurs. Now, I really didn't know where to go for help.

One cold late February morning in 1993, I watched a golf infomercial promoting the hidden power in the wrists and hands. Suddenly, it dawned on me that I never paid attention to what my hands were doing as I made contact with the ball. That's because the use of hands was a taboo thought, one of the don't dos in golf instruction. There was no question that my hands didn't turn over naturally the way the pros said they should, and the way I saw every pro in slow motion. Then the light bulb then went off in my mind like a lightening bolt from the sky. What other body part actually touches the club except the hands, and what makes more sense than using the hands to control the club as it strikes the ball?

After seeing the pro demonstrating different gadgets, designed to set the wrists and fire the hands at the ball, I was anxious to try it out for myself. As the season began I experimented with methods to use my hands and wrists, along with the swing. Also, I focused my concentration on solid ball striking, compared to just making a powerful swing, like before. I over exaggerated the flapping and hinging of the wrists, but the results spoke for themselves, as my ball striking improved and the distance increased. This was definitely the beginning of finding the fix I searched long and hard for. What amazed me the most was how easily I now hit a draw with my irons, like I never could before. Still, my ball striking was inconsistent. For another year, I experimented with many methods to square the club and repeat the motion. The missing piece was finding the magical swing-thought that would make it happen, on demand.

The long awaited day came quite innocently in July 1995. Upon taking an afternoon break; I headed to the club with my pitching wedge. Before each round I typically warmed up by chipping balls into the practice bunker, thirty yards away. On the first shot I took a short backswing, but decided to try my new wrist action as I struck the ball. Instead of landing inside or short like it had over the past few seasons, the ball jumped off the club and flew twenty yards beyond. On the second try the results were the same.

My immediate thought was WOW, did that feel good! My next was, what did I just do? There was a startled look on my face when I discovered my hands were rotating into impact. Also, I ended up in the classic power position after the swing, just like I wanted to. Because I took such a short and slow motion type swing, I could clearly see what the hands were doing. I noticed that my top hand was making a motion, I could only describe as making a *Thumbs Down* at the golf ball. More importantly, this motion magically squared the club and was easy for me to repeat with every shot that followed.

It was golf euphoria, as I raced to the driving range to try it with full swings. Immediately I began hitting the ball solid and longer with every club, but now with a right to left draw like never before. My confidence returned as the *Thumbs Down* method gave me an ability to hit and control shots like I wanted to, but couldn't for a long time.

As I began using the *Thumbs Down* method on the course, I discovered the next challenge was the mental part of the process. As a lifetime fader or slicer of the ball I always aimed left of the target. Because the slice was now replaced with a draw, I had to aim straight, or slightly right of the target. It wasn't easy trusting my new ball flight, because now the ball is going in the opposite direction of where I remember. Now when I lined up a shot, I aimed toward the same area I was previously trying to avoid. Regardless, it was a problem I was happy to deal with.

On each shot, I needed to convince myself that making a *Thumbs Down* at impact would make the ball go where I wanted it to. My confidence increased, because more often than not, it did. The *Thumbs Down* method was now a regular part of my golf swings. My ball striking improved as I tweaked and made slight adjustments with my hands. At the beginning, I used the same grip as when I sliced, but over hooked the ball. To straighten it out, I gradually adjusted my left hand on my grip until I got it right. With just a simple adjustment, no more slice and no more over hooking the ball. It thrilled me, as I thought of the huge opportunities my simple method could create. I had discovered the missing ingredient the experts didn't want us to know about. It offered benefits for millions of amateurs around the world and busy people using the golf course for business.

The *Thumbs Down* method provided me with these main benefits, when I added it to my existing swing:

- A power booster I could use with any club

- A swing guide I could follow in my head on every shot

- The mental pictures I painted in my mind allowed me to replay the lessons, anywhere, anytime

Now that I knew I had something that worked for me, I needed a test case to try it out on. The following week, I was playing with someone who had the same fading ball flight as I did. Even better, he recently took a lesson from our assistant pro, so this would prove to a great initial test.

At the practice range after the round, he hit a few drives without me showing him anything. This way I could make a before and after comparison. Just like on the course he struck them well, but all weakly faded or sliced to the right. I explained how I fixed my slice by making changes with my hands, and then demonstrated the *Thumbs Down* method. I told him to hit the next one making a *Thumbs Down* motion while striking the ball. His first shot took off on a straight line, then drew slightly to the left. After his next shot drew strong to the left again I said, "did you see the same thing I just saw"? Although he shared my enthusiasm with the results, he disagreed with the reason why. I knew he was brainwashed because he'd taken many lessons where the instructor stressed swing mechanics, like a pro. He believed he'd just made better swings. I knew better.

What I discovered by watching golf for over thirty-years was, a pretty swing don't mean a thing. It was more important to strike the ball like the pros do, then trying to swing like them. My own ball striking problems were solved by thinking in the reverse order of what was being taught. Because I wasn't a pro or perceived expert, I quickly realized it wouldn't be embraced kindly by golf instructors and pros. My efforts to promote the *Thumbs Down* method would be challenging to say the least.

In 1997, my career was floundering. One day, I looked out at the course and saw how many players I thought would benefit by using the *Thumbs Down* method. At that moment, I decided to write a "how-to" book designed for the masses, because I knew nothing like this was currently available on the market. At least if it was, I never found it and it never found me.

Harvey Penick, one of the master instructors of golf had a book of ideas he taught to top pros called "The Little Red Book". It's small size and red color served as a great model. What I liked was that it could fit into a golf bag and the color could easily be remembered during practiced sessions, or while playing. I didn't want to compete head-on against books and training aids written by pros or master instructors. To compete in the market, the *Thumbs Down* method not only had to work as advertised, my book had to help amateurs improve their ball striking, without looking like a book.

In contrast to the technical information I read, I wanted to let pictures tell most of the story. Over time, I compiled dozens of pictures from magazines showing the best male and female players from all eras, in the perfect impact (*Thumbs Down*) position. Since my brother-in-law was a talented artist I asked him to re-draw a few pictures of these pros, versus using pictures of me. The format included simple explanations that highlighted their use of the *Thumbs Down* method, regardless of what they said they were doing.

The last major question was how could I publish a book without going broke in the process? I wanted something I could create for under a dollar on my word processor and reproduce on a copier. Because I liked the red book color concept, a bright orange cover was selected, with an idea to attach it to the golf bag, like a bag tag. This made it portable for use at the practice range, plus visible to use as a mental reminder on the golf course. Instead of just being just another book, it was now a virtual golf lesson you could take anywhere and use any time, legally under the rules of golf. This concept allowed me to position it as an on-course training aid, demanding more money than a book written by an amateur could get. It was a plan.

At the beginning of the project, I expected it to take about a year to complete. The challenges quickly surfaced, as I saw how difficult it was to combine graphics and words on such a small page, using a word processor. To embed the pictures I'd shrink the artist's drawings, cut and paste them into a blank space, then make a copy. After two stressful years, I found ways to shrink down the content by highlighting only the key points. Soon I was producing samples of the book's first half, a major accomplishment. It made me proud to hand them out and take pre-orders for the completed version. My friends were happy to pay the $20 I was asking.

The second half was much more difficult. Many years had already passed since 1995, when *Thumbs Down* became a regular part of my vocabulary. Trying to follow the original intent of creating a How-To guide, with drills an amateur could practice and teach himself or herself, became a challenge to re-create. Little-by-little it came together, as I worked throughout the summer, often times by the pool at the pool-club in town. On the day of the World Trade Center attacks in 2001, I was in the process of making my first official book presentation to a potential sponsor, when his wife called twice within twenty minutes. After the second call, the presentation was over and the world as we knew it changed forever.

Later in September, the second half was completed and the book was finally finished. Four years, ten months and twenty-three days from start to finish. I never thought the recent events were an omen meant for me, but the first reviews of my book weren't very good. People I showed it to liked the *Thumbs Down* method idea, but often criticized the way it read.

After the new-year I called one of my test players, a family friend who raved about how the *Thumbs Down* method improved his ball striking. He had lots of money and agreed to finance the printing of 3,000 books, now called the Preview edition, for distribution at golf outings. A company in that business offered me an opportunity to include books in the goody bags at their tournaments throughout 2002, but for free. I included a special offer for investors and one for anyone that wanted the full book.

At least with a finished product, I could now concentrate on sales, marketing and PR. In March of 2003 I met the editor of a golf magazine at local golf show who liked the *Thumbs Down* move for his struggling game. As we hit balls one August evening while I taught him the *Thumbs Down* method, he began taking pictures and decided to publish my first article in his September edition. It offered a $5 special, and produced my first seven sales that year. Again, I wasn't encouraged with the lack of interest and the criticism I received.

After a bad Wednesday at work the following June, I read the local paper's weekly golf page. Feeling down with the fear of losing my job again, I tried to ignite my new career as an author by calling the sportswriter. Surprised, he answered the phone and quickly liked my story, offering to come to my house the following Saturday and publish the article in the next week's edition. Beginning early on the Wednesday morning it came out, my phone rang with hungry golfers calling to order. In total, the article produced over $400 worth of orders, a new record. Both articles proved to me how effective the media was for creating sales, not just interest. It also showed me that golfers would impulsively spend over $20 if they thought it would help them to improve.

At the annual golf show in 2006 I took a booth to begin promoting the *Thumbs Down* method. By this time the book had gone through major changes and improvements, influenced by years of input. Each year thousands of everyday golfers attended this Friday through Sunday event. On Saturday, a reporter from a monthly publication came by and expressed interest in doing a story. We met the following May at a driving range, as he interviewed me for the June edition. I enjoyed reading the two-page story, which produced many new book customers again.

The question of whether or not the *Thumbs Down* method was a real invention came up many times during the interview, because it wasn't a gadget like most other inventions. All my life I wanted to invent something new in the world of sports, and being able to call myself an inventor would be one of life's highlights. I told the reporter that since the definition of an invention is something new, created for the purposes of solving a problem, the *Thumbs Down* method qualified. It was a unique solution I created to solve my slicing problem.

I also believed it was more than just an invention. I was confident that with the right exposure, the *Thumbs Down* method had potential to be something big in the world of golf. As if it was scripted, one morning in December as I watched the Golf Channel, they played a promotional message asking the question "do you think you have the next big idea in golf"? They were planning a show to showcase the best new golf inventions, with auditions in a few selected US cities beginning in mid-January. You can imagine my surprise to see this. I immediately looked at the TV and decided it was time to find out if I had something real, or not. Next, I went online and saw an audition date in the New York area in February, then submitted an application and waited for further instructions.

When I arrived at the hotel for the audition on the first of February, I registered as number sixty-one in a growing line that continued throughout the day. A total of 125 fellow wannabe's presented their inventions for three minutes each, to a producer and cameraman. My turn finally came just after 12:00. I felt I was prepared, but since I didn't have a gadget like everyone else, I wasn't confident. Just in case, I decided to leave a copy of the book for the producer to read on the trip home.

The website said it could take a month to find out which 100 inventions were selected to compete in the finals, March 24-26 in Orlando. What a thrill when I got the call on the first of March, telling me that my invention was selected. The Golf Channel invited me to audition again on March 25. No matter what the final outcome, I felt like a winner. The *Thumbs Down* method was officially an invention. Also, there was the remote possibility of becoming the next big thing in golf, just like I dreamed.

Early that morning when I learned that the panel of experts consisted of two pros and a professional instructor, I knew my chances to advance in the competition were finished. Just as I had predicted ten years earlier, it only took thirty seconds to confirm that pros didn't like it. One by one, they questioned the validity of my invention, saying the method was sound, but what's new about it? When they told me they used it themselves and complimented the fact that the method was fundamentally correct, I decided not to fight back and explain how new it really was. After all, other than myself who else in golf uses the term *Thumbs Down*? So far, no one I've seen. Three *Thumbs Down*'s by the judges and I was eliminated, but not broken.

The following week I attended the National Publicity Summit in New York City. I was selected as one of only one hundred authors and entrepreneurs from around the world, to meet the media one-on-one during a three-day event. Thanks to the Summit, I found the publisher I was looking for and appeared on a morning TV show, as the golf and business expert.

To top off my 2007 year, the Golf Channel appearance opened the door for me to appear on Inside Golf, a weekly golf show I frequently watched. The segment featured The *Thumbs Down* method, as I improved the producer's ball striking and cured his slice, live. This was the final test that confirmed the method worked, as advertised. Many viewers purchased my eBook immediately following the show. The producer was so impressed; he gave me a repeat performance a few weeks later. Again, the amateurs got the message, as many new customers purchased my products, complimenting the simplicity of the *Thumbs Down* method.

More than ten years after my mission of love began, the original How-To guide concept has matured into a trilogy of editions. I'm now in my fifties, working hard to start a new career as a full-time author and entrepreneur, in the fields of golf and marketing. Thanks to the Internet and technology I now have eBooks, videos, plus online virtual coaching sessions to offer.

I love what I do everyday. Now, when I'm thinking about, watching or playing golf, I'm also working. You could say I'm living The American Dream. At least I can say I'm showing up everyday and giving it my best shot.

"Fore"word

The Most Important Round of your Golfing Life Follows

GET READY FOR some outside-the-box thinking for improving your golf game. You probably never thought of *Thumbs Down*® as a positive thing, but now it is. In fact, this negative expression is the best thing that ever happened to your ball striking, and possibly your entire golf game.

Believe me, it's not just another gimmick. Making a *Thumbs Down* motion while striking the golf ball squares the club and provides a power booster to your existing swing, without trying to kill the ball. It increases clubhead speed, releases the club and puts you into the correct finishing position, like magic.

Let's face it, we're all busy and lessons take a commitment in time and money. For some, it's the perfect way to learn the golf swing, gain valuable tips and discover ways to improve your game from an experienced professional. If the amount of time and money it takes to play the game is already a stretch, which is not uncommon with today's fast-paced lifestyles, then a self-teaching handbook may be the answer you've been looking for. It was for me.

My name is Alan Martin, a single-digit handicap golfer. The power fade, which served me well for twenty-five years, had turned into an out-of-control slice during the early 1990s. I struggled and searched for a simple solution to correct the slice, but never found it. In 1995, while experimenting with ways to get the club square at impact, I developed a method, which was simple and easy to repeat. Better yet, it didn't require changing my swing, just some adjustments to my hand position at impact and changes to my thinking.

The method, called *Thumbs Down*, is based on the same swing fundamentals taught by the best instructors, in a language the average golfer actually understands and can relate to. For me the results were dramatic. It immediately turned the slice into a draw, plus added well over twenty yards to every club in my bag (putter excluded). My game now includes a level of accuracy and control I never knew before.

Thumbs Down: Golf Instruction Made Simple was designed to be a unique How-To guide and training aid. The subject matter was designed by me, not a pro. It teaches you How-To teach yourself, using the *Thumbs Down* method I developed to fix my slice.

My intended audience is fellow amateur golfers who want to improve with a passion, male or female, young or old. The Front Nine is a Preview that intro-duces the *Thumbs Down* method. The Back Nine comes complete with ball striking drills that teach you How-To square the club at impact and maximize every club in your bag (putter excluded). Each drill focuses on the moments just before and just after the club makes contact with the ball.

 You'll quickly improve driving distance and accuracy, plus develop the feel for controlling shots within 100 yards, where the real scoring is done.

Simply put: more distance, more fairways, more greens, more often.

LOWER SCORES ARE NOT A GUARANTEE
they are the natural results.

Welcome

DO YOU KNOW ME? I'm one of the main characters in *Thumbs Down: Golf Instruction Made Simple*.

Throughout this book you'll see ME in many classic poses that show you what all the best players do, not what they say they do. Every picture tells a story that shows you where to set your golf swing priorities and focus your concentration.

○ Learn How-To improve your ball striking, maximize your practice time and enjoy the game more.

○ Get a visual checklist that reinforces these fundamentals and more: The proper grip, posture, ball striking positions, alignment and swing path.

Don't be fooled! The golfers you see aren't the real me, your author. They're actually an all-star team of golf's best men's and ladies' professionals from many eras. All were recreated by an artist and disguised as either ME or SHE.

> These great pros demonstrate my method of squaring the club called *Thumbs Down*, which any golfer can learn and execute in minutes.

The Problem

IN ORDER TO IMPROVE, the average golfer needs simple answers to his or her simple questions, but rarely gets them.

THE FAQS from amateur golfers of all levels of play — which one (or more) of these is your favorite?

- How should I swing to square the club at impact?

- How should I swing to correct my slice?

- How should I swing to play a draw?

- How should I swing to become a more consistent ball striker?

- How do I get my swing back "on plane"?

- How should I swing to hit more accurate shots, more often?

- What drills should I practice to square the club?

- What's the best way to warm-up in the few minutes before tee-off time?

See how many of these questions refer to the golf swing and imply that you need to change it for different shots.

The Solution

DON'T CHANGE YOUR SWING. Instead, make a strong, controlled swing and learn How-To square the clubface as it strikes the ball.

SQUARING THE CLUB AT IMPACT
Why is it so important?

- The entire golf swing takes two seconds or less.

- During an entire round, the club makes contact with the ball for less than two seconds **total**.

WARNING!

The information that follows will cause permanent damage to these flaws (and others) in your golf game.

These were the short list of my own problems. All were the result of my inability to get the club squared at impact:

○ Out of control slice.

○ Weak, fading shots to the green.

○ Inconsistent driving distance and accuracy.

○ A lack of feel in the short game.

○ Difficulty with shot making from 100 yards and in.

○ Lost confidence, controlling where the ball is going.

IF THE CLUB ISN'T SQUARE
your shots could end up anywhere.

To fix my own problems, the natural place to look for a simple solution was in golf publications, following the advice given by the best instructors and pros in the game. Their articles and lessons provided volumes of useful and credible information, but what I found was that applying the tips at the practice range was both frustrating and counter-productive.

What I really needed was a How-To guide complete with step-by-step drills to practice, that would provide positive results each practice session. Unfortunately, no such guide existed at that time.

As we all know, golf is a complex game. The golf swing consists of a never ending list of steps, all important and all executed in just split seconds. To the best players, squaring the club at impact is natural, literally taken for granted. Their swing fundamentals are so solid they can afford to focus their attention on perfecting the finer details of the golf swing. For the rest us there's nothing natural about it.

The majority of amateur golfers slice. The *Thumbs Down* method was originally created to cure my slice. To this day I'm still amazed at how simple the fix really was. Any golfer that already knows how to hit the golf ball will see noticeable results within minutes using the *Thumbs Down* method. Focus your practice time mastering the method, then watch your golf swing magically get better, all by itself.

THUMBS DOWN DRAMATICALLY IMPROVED MY GOLF GAME
by changing an out-of-control slice into a draw, almost overnight.

A Pretty Swing Don't Mean a Thing...

Unless the club is squared at impact

IT'S TIME TO FOCUS on the portion of the golf swing that can yield the most dramatic improvements to your game (putting excluded).

The information to follow highlights the portion of the golf swing too many instructors glance over, the moment just before the club makes contact with the ball.

Simply put, **this is the portion of a pro's swing you need to copy**.

Let's now look at two of today's most overlooked and misunderstood fundamentals for consistent ball striking:

1. Top hand position

2. Top hand rotation through the impact zone

WARNING!

This is a controversial subject. Expect it to be interpreted as radical thinking by many.

Thumbs Down is a simple method any player can quickly learn. It squares the club with your existing swing, plus **adds an extra pop on the ball without over swinging**. Based on many of the same swing fundamentals taught by the best instructors *Thumbs Down* **makes better ball striking easier than you ever imagined.**

BETTER GOLF, MORE OFTEN
The bottom line.

Ball Striking 101
Hit it like a pro

AS THE EXPRESSION GOES, if you want to get really good at something copy a pro. Do what they do!

The best players from all pro tours; mens, ladies and champions, have golf swings which are unique not always pretty. What they have in common is all make the same active hands motion as they strike down on the ball. So should you!

THE MOST IMPORTANT SPLIT SECOND OF THE GOLF SWING IS RIGHT NOW,
just prior to impact.

ROTATE YOUR TOP HAND NOW

Turn your *Thumbs* to point *Down* at the ball as you strike down on it.

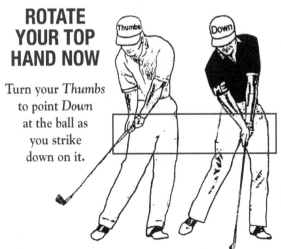

The *Thumbs Down* motion squares the golf club at impact...

and puts it into the ideal hitting position as it strikes the ball.

PROS ARE GREAT BALL STRIKERS
Great ball strikers have great hand action.

Thumbs are a key for better golf.

Good putters use their thumbs for feel, also to visualize the line. Use your thumbs to improve your ball striking too.

It's showtime, a split second to impact. **Do you know where your thumbs are?** It should come as no surprise that most amateurs don't have a clue.

Because the hands are the only part of your body that comes in contact with the golf club, it's critical to understand and control what the hands are doing when you strike the ball.

THUMBS ARE THE TRIGGERS that unleash the power in your hands, wrists and forearms.

Combining *Thumbs Down* with your current swing provides **A VIRTUAL SWING GUIDE**

+

A POWER BOOSTER generating tremendous clubhead speed at impact.

THE BEST KEPT SECRET FOR BETTER BALL STRIKING

The power of the thumbs.

Thumbs Down for Thumbs Up Results

ALTHOUGH THEIR SWINGS all look different, this image shows what pros and low handicappers have in common:

Their hands end up in this position just after impact.

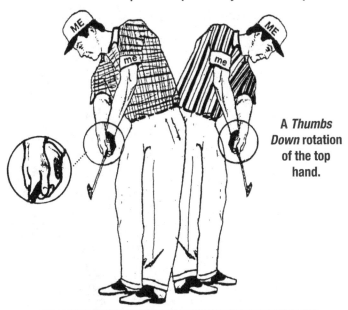

A *Thumbs Down* rotation of the top hand.

This picture clearly reveals the *Thumbs Down* position just after striking the ball.

MAKE THIS YOUR NEW SWING PRIORITY

Start Thinking Like ME

A Champion's Champion in the classic **L** position. The golf swing doesn't really begin until it reaches this position on your downswing.

Master this zone when you practice.

Start With Solid Ball Contact
and work backwards

YOUR TOP PRIORITIES for better ball striking need to be striking down on the ball with the clubface square. Because golf is a game of feel it's critical for amateurs to frequently experience the feel of hitting the ball on the club's sweet spot. Next, develop your swing to consistently deliver the club online to the ball. Arguably this is in the wrong order from what's commonly taught today.

Refer to the player on the previous page. His swing has reached the position where the hands are near waist height, a zone referred to as the slot. Use this area as a checkpoint to feel the club's position on the downswing into the impact zone.

Remember: you can't hit the ball during the first 3/4 of your swing, so don't try to. Instead: keep your swing under control as you reach the slot, then accelerate into the impact zone on the your downswing.

A common mistake made by amateurs (your author sometimes included) is they try to kill every shot. All too often they begin accelerating from the top of the downswing. This motion makes the shoulders come down first and cut across the ball. The typical result: a wicked slice or even worse.

3/4 OF THE GOLF SWING IS PREPARATION TO IMPACT
Don't over swing!

Keeping it simple isn't always easy.

Learning a reliable, repeatable method is all too often confusing, time consuming and expensive, plus it often requires a swing change. Not anymore.

For increased *distance, accuracy and control* ALL IT TAKES are these two subtle moves added to your existing swing:

○ Set your hands on the takeaway.   ○ Fire them down on the ball.

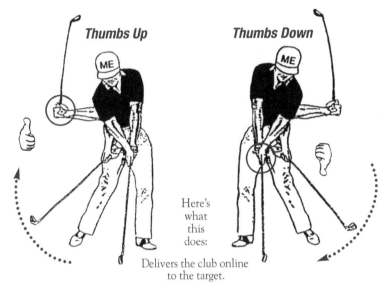

Thumbs Up   *Thumbs Down*

Here's
what
this
does:

Delivers the club online
to the target.

○ Prepares the hands on the takeaway.

○ Hinges the wrists on the backswing.

○ Increases clubhead speed.

○ Strikes the ball with an extra pop.

IN THE GAME OF GOLF
it doesn't get any easier than this.

Timing is Everything
especially for better ball striking

AS YOU'RE LOOKING DOWN at the ball, visualize it as a clock.

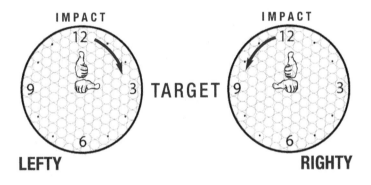

The pictures show that your strong hand thumb should be pointing to 12:00 at the moment of impact (squaring the club). Then it rotates to 3:00 (the target) if you're a lefty or to 9:00 (the target) if you're a righty.

Rotate *Thumbs Down* with the same motion you'd make with a screwdriver, to loosen or to tighten a screw that's in the ground.

Lefties: Tighten
Clockwise

Righties: Loosen
Counterclockwise

Try this drill. Place your hands together as if you're gripping the golf club. Make this motion with an accelerated, snapping action when striking the golf ball. As you accelerate into impact your thumbs will naturally rotate toward 6:00. That's to be expected.

At first this motion may feel wristy and awkward, but over time it will turn smooth and rhythmic.

IT'S ABOUT TIME
You can do this.

MAKE IT HAPPEN
by rotating your forearms.

A simple turning motion with the top thumb (counterclockwise for righties or clockwise for lefties) makes your wrists rollover the same as the best players do.

This rotation is the missing ingredient in the golf
swings of the majority of amateur golfers…

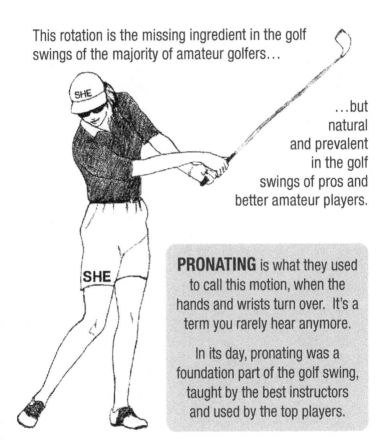

…but
natural
and prevalent
in the golf
swings of pros and
better amateur players.

PRONATING is what they used
to call this motion, when the
hands and wrists turn over. It's a
term you rarely hear anymore.

In its day, pronating was a
foundation part of the golf swing,
taught by the best instructors
and used by the top players.

THUMBS DOWN SIMPLIFIES THIS
*making it easy to execute, repeat
and remember.*

LET'S REVIEW THE BASICS.

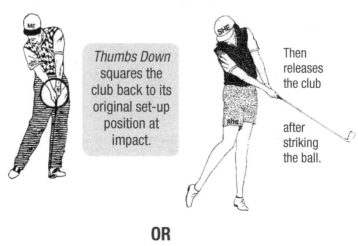

Thumbs Down squares the club back to its original set-up position at impact.

Then releases the club

after striking the ball.

OR

Striking Down on the ball

The Natural Release

THUMBS: The training aid you can practice with, *then legally use on the course during your round.*

Simplicity at Last

THE DRILLS THAT FOLLOW were designed to make it easy for any golfer to develop the feel for consistently hitting solid shots, online to the target. They let you practice whenever you want wherever you are, with or without a club.

In just minutes you can learn to execute *Thumbs Down*, my training method that squares the golf club and simplifies ball striking. The *Thumbs Down* method benefits players of all skill levels.

You'll quickly learn How-To:

- Square the club at impact.
- Improve your ball striking.
- Develop swing memory.
- Visualize and repeat your good swings.
- Release the club through impact.
- Practice more effectively.
- Accelerate your rate of improvement.

**ONE METHOD
PROVIDES ALL THESE BENEFITS
AND MORE**

Final Word

IN THE 21ST CENTURY, playing a better game of golf is easier than ever before. After all, the explosion of golf has produced numerous improvements in equipment, teaching aids and ways to improve your game. Manufacturers are using technology to build lighter and stronger clubs with larger sweet spots, made from titanium and other space age alloys.

Computer aided designs produce balls with superior aero-dynamics, making them fly longer with more accuracy, stopping on a dime. High tech training aids, swing machines, reminder grips and guides for firming your wrists are all available from pros and master instructors. Golf schools are growing in leaps and bounds. Lessons are now available regularly on TV, computer and MP3 format. Every golf tournament has a segment offering tips.

These examples are only a sampling of the many tools available to make your golf swing virtually automatic. Today's choices are almost endless. Equipment manufacturers guarantee lower scores or your money back (less shipping and handling of course). With all these options available, the game is only getting easier.

We only wish.

The moral of this story is simple. *Thumbs Down*, for Thumbs Up results.

Are You Ready to Take Your Game to the Next Level?

If you're tired of searching for:

○ A simple way to improve your game, in minutes.

○ The ideal gift for the serious golfer who has everything.

○ A unique promotional product and corporate gift, that leaves a positive lasting impression.

It's time to stop searching!

The Front Nine introduced a new and unique method that cured my slice, called *Thumbs Down*. My revolutionary guide for better ball striking was designed for amateurs, with foundation information that focuses on squaring the club at impact, as the #1 priority of the golf swing.

The Front Nine sponsor's edition is a unique promotional product and corporate gift. Customize the back cover with your logo and personal message.

The Back Nine is your How-To guide. Maximize your practice time. Teach Yourself the *Thumbs Down* method, in minutes. Includes:

- Power booster

- Swing guide

- Drills

- Do's and Don'ts

- On-course training aid bag tag, (just pay $4 S&H)

Get them both in **The Pro edition**. It's an e-Book that combines the Front and Back Nines. Includes: Video download, PLUS a 30-minute one-on-one virtual lesson with Alan Martin.

BONUS OFFERS:

- 100% trade-in value: Purchase the Pro edition and get back 100% of what you paid for the Front Nine. (proof of purchase price required)

- FREE video download

- FREE on-course training aid bag tag. (just pay $4 S&H)

○ $19.97 "virtual lesson" membership (per month). Save over $200 per month (includes: bVisual, on-line virtual meeting subscription)

For more information visit:
www.ThumbsDownMethod.com/offers

CPSIA information can be obtained
at www.ICGtesting.com
Printed in the USA
JSHW011401100920
7768JS00002B/212